MELODIOUS
ACCORD
Good Singing in Church

Alice Parker

MELODIOUS
ACCORD
Good Singing in Church

Liturgy Training Publications

ACKNOWLEDGMENTS

This is the second in a series of small books on music and liturgy. The first is *How Can I Keep from Singing?* by Gabe Huck.

The title of this book, *Melodious Accord*, is taken from a metrical version of Psalm 100 made by James Montgomery, "His praise with melodious accordance prolong." It is also the name of a nonprofit organization founded by Alice Parker in 1985. This membership group looks at the art of music as a whole in our society and seeks to let song bring people together in both sacred and secular settings. Melodious Accord presents professional workshops, a fellowship program, a composition search, and sponsors Alice Parker's appearances around the country. Information is available from Melodious Accord, 801 West End Avenue, 9-D, New York NY 10025; 212/663-1165.

Quotation sources. Abraham Joshua Heschel, *The Insecurity of Freedom* (New York: Schocken Books, 1959). • Dorothy Sayers, "Toward a Christian Aesthetic," in *The Whimsical Christian* (New York: Macmillan, 1979). • Eric A. Havelock, *The Muse Learns to Write* (New Haven: Yale University Press, 1986). • George Steiner, *A Reader* (New York: Oxford University Press, 1984). • Dorothy Sayers, *The Mind of the Maker*, (New York: Harper & Row, 1968). • John Wesley, "Directions for Singing," *Methodist Hymnal*, 1964. • St. Bernard, quoted in "Robert Lawlor: Geometry at the Service of Prayer," *Parabola*, 3:1, 16. • Nikolaus Harnoncourt, *Baroque Music Today: Music as Speech* (Portland: Amadeus Press, 1988).

Cover and design: Jill Smith

Art: Linda Ekstrom

Liturgy Training Publications, 1800 North Hermitage Avenue, Chicago IL 60622-1101; 1-800-933-1800; FAX 1-800-933-7094

ISBN 0-929650-43-3

CONTENTS

CHAPTER

1

The Need for
Song

Are your people singing?

CHURCH MUSICIAN: *I can't hear them. But I can see: They stand, and don't open their mouths.*

What have you done about it?

We've tried rehearsing before the service. We put information in the bulletin. And, of course, the choir and organ are helping.

Is there ever a time when they do sing?

Only when the music is really familiar. Then it's loud, but not in any way musical.

Do you think they could sing well?

I don't know. It would take a lot of time and work—and maybe a miracle!

Do you think they can sing well if you don't expect them to?

I'm supplying all the help I can.

But if you don't have a "vision" of congregational sound, you have no way to recognize the difference between what you are getting and what you could be asking for. Somehow, in music, you get exactly what you ask for, and no more.

I get good results from my choir. Don't I just have to take what I can get from untrained voices?

Congregations are different from choirs. And one of the mysteries of music and of other disciplines is that different leaders get different results from the same group. Good conductors don't just "take what they can get": They project their vision. If they are skilled in the combining of craft and vision, the people respond.

But it helps to have singers who know how to read.

No. Reading is visual. Music is aural. They are very different. Nonreaders can sing wonderfully well "by ear," as we find in folk musicians all over the world.

But we're not singing folk music.

The human equation is the same. Do your people want to sing?

What do you mean?

I think that you don't expect enough of your congregation. You see them as a musically apathetic group, when you could see them as possessing ears, voices, minds, hearts and a common heritage. That's all that we need to make music.

Do you think a congregation is supposed to make beautiful music?

That's just what I think! Some can, but none can do better until their leader expects them to do better.

You mean I'm holding them back?

In a word, yes! You know your music, but you've not thought about how to draw song out of people.

MY OWN IDEA of what a congregation might be asked to do changed radically after I heard Mennonite singing in the late 1950s. One voice began a familiar hymn. On the second note, the entire room joined in the most beautiful four-part hymn singing I had ever heard. It gave me a vision of what hymn singing must have been in days past and could be again in days to come.

It made me realize that where there is an unbroken tradition of good singing, children grow up hearing their parents and neighbors sing and recognizing that they love to sing. It is the norm. They simply join in.

In our age and culture, that continuity has been broken. Many children never hear their parents sing. They grow up valuing only the sounds that come from some electronic device. If they do get taken to church, they are often ignored by all the grown-ups. They don't hear hymns or other service music at home. Many don't get any music training in school or in religious education classes. If children have never heard good group singing by people they know and love, they can't have any idea of what they are missing.

As the Mennonites demonstrated, it was not always thus. From all periods of music history, and from contemporary experiences in Third World cultures, we see how music is a vital and honored part of worship. I have seen a videotape of a Mass at a church in Malawi, where the music of the entrance rite took 20 minutes. People would not stop singing and dancing—everyone in the room—until the impulse had played itself out. We've moved far from participating in that energy released when we give ourselves to the song. We restrict the time allowed (one hour), the space (immovable furniture) and the body ("Sit still and be quiet!"). We do need quiet—a listening silence is the frame for music—but quiet should come as the balance for activity, music as the balance for speech, sitting still as the balance for lively bodily participation.

THERE ARE CHURCHES in all denominations in this country where congregations do sing well, and it is always because there is at least one person who is actively expecting it. This happy result is due mainly to the self-taught skills of the leaders: Little in their religious or artistic training has focused on this aspect of their work. Most of them get music simply because—in addition to doing all their homework—they love music and they expect music.

We need to rethink our training of church music leaders, with the first priority given to raising expectations about congregational singing. The congregational voice is the heart of all church music. It can and should be beautiful, meaningful, musical, full of the Spirit, responsive both to text and tune, and magnetic in drawing together all who hear.

The fathers desired that music should always abide in the church. That is why there are so many songs and psalms. This precious gift has been bestowed on us alone to remind us that we are created to praise and magnify the Lord.

—Martin Luther

CHAPTER 2

Good Singing Forges Good Congregations

What's important in church music?

CHURCH MUSICIAN: *It sets an atmosphere of worship. And singing the text is different from reading it. The congregation can join in, and the choir and organ add variety and color.*

Is music's only justification the accompaniment to text, or as contrast to the spoken word? Has it no religious value of its own?

What would that be?

Listen to Abraham Joshua Heschel: "Listening to great music is a shattering experience, throwing the soul into an encounter with an aspect of reality to which the mind can never relate itself adequately. Such experiences undermine conceit and complacency and may even induce a sense of contrition and a readiness for repentance. I am neither a musician nor an expert on music. But the shattering experience of music has been a challenge to my thinking on ultimate issues. I spend my life working with thoughts. And one problem that gives me no rest is: do these thoughts ever rise to the heights reached by authentic music?"

Melodious
Accord

AN ESKIMO CREATION STORY starts: "In the beginning was the Sound."

The premise of this small volume is that sound is a marvelous gift of God and that when we sing together in common—whether in joy or desolation or everyday hope—we affirm our common humanity and build our community through this shared craft. Good singing is not the result of a good congregation but the forging of it. No other gift connects us in quite this way.

Think for a moment about the physical properties of sound. Tones are produced by the vibration of air or water (thunder, wind, stream), strings or membranes (violin, drum), birds, animals or humans. These tones strike the ear. The ear's wondrously convoluted folds receive the vibrations and transmit them to the mind and heart.

Through singing and speaking we communicate with other humans and animals and perhaps, as in the old myths, with rocks, trees and stars. We converse with the entire universe of which we are part. Some scientists speak of vibration as at the heart of all physical processes, so it may be literally true that "All nature sings, and round me rings, The music of the spheres" (Maltbie D. Babcock).

We do not know how music provokes its effects on us. It stimulates responses that are different both in quality and extent from those of speech. Like other gifts of God, we can choose to use song wisely or dangerously, creatively or destructively, cherishing it or devaluing it.

OUR SOCIETY TENDS to think of music as either entertainment or advertising. British theologian—and mystery writer—Dorothy Sayers wrote well on this:

> The amusement art [is] the enjoyment of the emotions that usually accompany experience without having had the experience. It does not reveal us to ourselves. . . . It is "wish fulfillment" or "escape" literature in the worst sense. Or take the spell-binding kind of art . . . [that] seeks to produce the behavior without the experience. In its vulgarest form it becomes pure propaganda. It can actually succeed in making its audience into the thing it desires to have them. . . . This pseudoart does not really communicate power to us; it merely exerts power over us.

"Amusement art" exists in church music also when that music draws on the clichés of popular music without contributing a musical identity of its own. ("We won't attract young people unless we give them what they want.")

And song as propaganda is found among us where the words take precedence over the music, as if, when the words say "God loves us," it doesn't matter whether the tune has any musical integrity.

In our society we have become separated from the way sound makes connections in the physical world and creates unity with the spiritual realm. The twentieth century seems to have brought vast separations. As scientific knowledge advances, and the world shrinks, we know less and less about relating to our neighbors and preserving communal activities.

We have almost forgotten how to listen. We are so eye-oriented that the page has become disassociated from the human sounds that gave it existence. We are so busy with page and screen that we fail to become part of the sound, to silence all activity except the sound-receptors, to become open to all that sound alone can tell us. Remember the Mianus Bridge on Interstate 95 at Greenwich, Connecticut? It cried out for six months before it collapsed. We didn't listen.

Native Americans have a saying:

> We teach our children
> to look
> when there is nothing to see
> to listen
> when there is nothing to hear.

There is always something to hear! Not necessarily what we expect to hear, or want to hear, but what sound itself can tell us if we value silence enough.

In brief, our rational minds have short-circuited our senses, so that we are not receiving the messages of wholeness, of sanity, of form and proportion, of balanced relationships, which the natural world is constantly sending us.

OUR SOCIETY IS perhaps the only one known to have separated the best music-making from religion and so to have allowed an inferior strain of functional music to usurp the place of all-uniting sound. It is interesting but fruitless to speculate on who initiated the divorce. In a way we are all responsible. The separation of music itself into different spheres—high art, academic, folk, pop, jazz, religious—is symptomatic of twentieth-century stresses.

The church must call for the remarriage of the best artistic minds with the best theological minds. We need to reunite what our senses tell us with what our rational minds devise; they complement one another. We need to redefine what music is in its physical, human and spiritual senses. We need to be clear about the human qualities of song—that it does not exist until incarnate in the human throat—and how to set up the conditions that make it possible. We need to value the song for what it alone can do.

16

Good Singing
Forges Good
Congregations

As for public prayers, there are two kinds: the one consists simply of speech, the other of song. . . . And indeed, we know from experience that singing has great strength and power to move and to set our hearts on fire in order that we may call upon God and praise him with a more vehement and more ardent zeal.

—John Calvin

CHAPTER 3

Ear and Eye

So, do you teach them how to read?

CHURCH MUSICIAN: *There's no time. There is always more music to learn.*

Isn't that self-defeating?

Well, these singers are just volunteers. They are giving their time and talent to the church. I can't ask them to do homework or to risk flunking a test!

And do they sing well, after you have taught them?

Yes, if it's a piece they know well and like. Of course, there's a vibrato problem, and intonation is apt to be low, and blend is difficult. But they do make a good choral sound.

Related to what? To vocal production? To the needs of the music? To the acoustical properties of the church? Are they improving as singers? Do they "make music"?

As church choirs go, they are good. But it's all I can do to get our music learned in time for the service. Voice lessons and instruction in musicianship would have to take place outside of rehearsal.

I think you might need to reexamine your priorities. Now you are teaching each piece note by note instead of teaching people to read well and musically. Have you ever thought of the opposite: of teaching them a song by rote so that they could sing beautifully in unison? Or of improvising simple settings on familiar hymns so they are liberated from the page? You could at least set up the expectation that people singing with you are going to learn and to grow both as musicians and as singers.

IN CURRENT EDUCATIONAL practice we accept without question the need for reading, almost as if all knowledge were imparted visually. But literacy came relatively late in human development. People lived and learned, spoke and sang for millennia before they learned to write and read.

Eric A. Havelock, in recounting the development of written language in Greek society, says in *The Muse Learns to Write:*

> [Vision] could never of itself create human society, nor our essential humanity. It is a fact of our biological inheritance that these emerged through the use of our ears and mouths.

Do we really use our ears and mouths, or are they dispensable in modern life? Is written language truly more important than listening and speaking? Havelock argues: "Was the text, as printed and multiplied . . . being robbed of any residual ability to 'speak'?"

It is in that kind of "speaking" that we need to be re-educated. And for such speaking we use the same physical equipment as for singing: ears to hear fine shadings of sound, lungs, larynx, vibrating cavities, and an expressive face and body that act together to "bring the old men from the chimney corner and keep the children from their play," as Sir Philip Sidney described the old, reciting poets. The storyteller, the bard, the aural poet creates a world in story or song and carries the listener into it. The Greek word *mousike* refers to poetry, song and dance all made memorable because of their intertwining. Havelock describes this unity:

> As you recited you sang; as you sang you played an instrument; as you played you danced, these motions being performed collectively. Their unusually sophisticated partnership supplied mutual reinforcement.

Our song leaders need just this kind of formation. People don't sing because they are "taught the notes." The vision of the poet and composer must leap off the page into living sound. The musically illiterate adult and the smallest child can and will respond to this kind of leadership, along with the rest of us who are sometimes so hampered by our training.

If I don't teach reading, or voice, or "the notes," what do I teach?

In a word, melody: that union of text and tune which can be expressed in each single voice without any accompaniment or setting.

Won't it confuse the basses to learn another part as well as the one they have to sing?

The bass, or any other part, is an adjunct to the melody. It does not exist independently. If the singers don't know the melody, they can't sing their parts well.

Usually the melody is the easiest part.

Exactly. It's what voices want to sing. Yet we don't take time to examine it in terms of sound, to sing it so that it captivates the singer and the listener.

Don't you just sing what's on the page?

Have you thought about the text: what it means, how it is expressed, its form, its use of idiom and metaphor? And how about the tune: the pitch and rhythmic elements, form, phrase and style? And how do they affect each other in performance?

IT HAS BEEN MANY YEARS since our schools taught Latin, asked children to memorize great poetry or Bible verses, required students to parse a sentence, or to steep themselves in the language of

Shakespeare and the King James Bible, those books which were read and re-read in frontier homes.

And with music: Who studies the forms of melody, the grammar of music? Who is steeped in the great single-line melodies of the past, to know how they are constructed, what makes them memorable, what ranges release voices, what rhythms tickle the ear and move the feet? Which church musicians listen to the sound that is actually happening, to learn how living voices interpret the page?

Or who studies the relationship of text and tune: the style or "voice" of the poem matched to that of the melody? Do these two voices reinforce or contrast? Is attention paid to the matching of accents and loaded syllables? Or who notices the pairing of an old tune with a new text (some can be wonderful), or a prayerful text to a jigging tune?

And who knows the history of music in melody, so that the era in which the song was first sung is re-created in our present singing? While there are historic and functional groups of melodies, in the best sense each tune is as unique as a person and needs to be sung with loving attention to its individual voice. I have written about this in a small volume entitled *Creative Hymn Singing* (Hinshaw Music, Inc., 1976). There I used familiar tunes and texts from six different periods, with ideas for their performance either as unison melodies or in improvised settings:

> A quick glance at the dates and geographic origins of the hymns demonstrates that there can be no such thing as one common hymn style. These tunes and texts are as diverse as the societies which produced them, and with a little imaginative effort, we can begin to re-create their original function and sound, and thereby make the music live again.

THESE MELODIES from the past have proved themselves. They have been sung by different generations, remembered and passed along, varied in many ways yet kept alive by their rightness. True folk music (unlike much of what has worn that name in the past few decades) expresses and transmits the essence of the society from which it sprang.

Ralph Vaughan Williams, himself an authority on English folklore, used a vivid paragraph from Gilbert

Murray to express these notions. Murray was referring to the Bible and the works of Homer:

> They have behind them not the imagination of one great poet, but the accumulated emotion, one may almost say, of the many successive generations who have read and learned and themselves fresh re-created the old majesty and loveliness. . . . There is in them, as it were, the spiritual life-blood of a people.

Authentic folk music is the expression of the soul of a people. And authentic composed music, resting securely on this concept of sound, is its expression through one individual imagination. This is the music we need in our churches: authentic folk music along with composed music that combines idea, craft and communicative power, songs that capture our language, concerns and "accumulated emotion."

Song is a right and a need. At certain times in history music has flooded into the church through great composers, poets and melodists. Such infusions inspire new growth. I'm certain that a new generation of great composers will arise not so much as a result of our technical teaching but from the nourishing of churches that sing well, that understand that music must feed our hearts and our souls as well as our minds.

Any thinking about the forms of meaning must grapple with music. . . . It is fair to say that our insights into the nature of music, . . . of the ways in which music comes to "possess" and affect our psyche, have not progressed decisively beyond Plato. . . . Music [is] the elect companion of identity, the homecoming to that inside oneself which time has in its keeping.

—George Steiner

CHAPTER | 4

Musical
Space and
Time

It seems difficult to talk about music with nonmusicians because our society thinks of music as something mysterious, otherworldly, rather than as a craft.

CHURCH MUSICIAN: *Do you mean like woodworking or fine baking?*

I particularly like the image of the potter. One plunges the hands into wet clay, starts the turning wheel and feels the impact of hand, gravity and motion on the mass which gradually assumes its shape.

Is the difficulty because we can't see or touch music?

Partly. But it's also because people are not familiar with the vocabulary we use. They can't believe that much of it is just expressing common sense.

I give up on such conversations much too soon.

Use a more creative response. Teach! Get people thinking of tones and time as if they were clay and wheel, the raw materials of art.

THE RAW MATERIAL of natural time (your pulse, day/night, moon, year) interacts with the raw material of the physics of sound (the vibrating of columns of air, of strings, of wood or stretched hide or anything that sounds). Martin Luther wrote: "There is nothing on earth that hath not its tone. Even the air invisible sings when smitten with a staff."

So there is time and there is vibration. The other physical principle at work is that of energy, the physics of motion. How does something get started, keep going, get stopped? The musician learns to channel the time/tone continuum into patterns that ride the currents of energy.

The best illustration I know is that of the sailor in an unmechanized sailboat who learns the lore of the sea by growing up in, on and at it. This sailor senses currents, tides, winds and weather. The response to the feel of the deck under foot, of the wind on the face and the sound of the sails above, is automatic, almost unconscious. The "old salt," sailing across the bay, works with the tide and wind to reach safe harbor with almost effortless precision.

The analogy in music is, I think, both in the appearance of simplicity and in the balancing of complex elements to achieve a clear goal.

Now that machines enable us to move through the water in a straight lines, have we lost the ability to "listen" to nature, to feel the deck, the wind, the tide? Our tape decks and CD players repeat the same performance over and over with none of the slight variation that is common to natural processes. We don't get a chance to learn how to listen to where the work is in its journey, to ride the moving currents, to align oneself with the energy.

If we apply this to group singing, we might ask: Does the song seem inevitable? Natural? Right? Does it flow from beginning to end? Do pitch and rhythm, text and form make one communicative whole? Is everyone caught in and affected by the music?

ANY MUSIC YOU HEAR is made up of time and tone and energy, but there is far more going on than physics. Music needs an initiator and a responder. It is a language sent and received, and for us as humans it is as varied as our human societies. Each aboriginal tribe developed its own language, customs, beliefs and art forms. In music, sounds of nature provided the model: wind and water, bird, fish, animal. Imitating these sounds, primitive people explored their own voices and body sounds, inventing instruments to extend the possibilities. (Flutes and drums of all kinds are common to early societies.) Humans have to learn through their senses, and the arts are exaltations of those senses.

In any society, pitches need to be tuned, true to their source and their context. That is, a clarinet "A" sounds different from a violin "A"—but either one needs to be carefully sounded to be right for the instrument and for the piece. And an "A" in one context (the time and place of first sounding) is different from each other context: A viol "A" is different from a violin "A" and a Bach "A" sounds different from a Stravinsky "A." They may all be vibrating 440 times a second, but the overtones and stylistic differences are acute and important. There is no such sound as a pure "A" outside a physics laboratory: The label is an abstraction: "A" needs re-creation—incarnation—to become living sound.

Rhythms also need to be timed, true to their source and the style of their context. The tempo (relative speed of the pulse) and meter (pulse plus accent) need to be just right for each individual piece. The tempo itself may be strict or free, or varying between the two; the meter may be strict or changing. Learning what belongs where is a lifetime's work.

THINK OF A SIMPLE MELODY like "Twinkle, twinkle little star" and see its notes ever so orderly on a staff. Now imagine a spiritual, say "Nobody knows the trouble I've seen." One of the characteristics of spirituals is the game that is played with both tones and beats. The great singer knowingly "bends" the pitch and anticipates or delays the beat, so that the music does not exactly conform to our rigid ways of writing music on the page. Both songs are music. Notation works better for the first than for the second.

Take this example one step further and imagine a little child singing "Twinkle," then an adult, then a pop singer, then an opera singer. The result in sound is totally different—and that difference is the music. And then the rhythm: Imagine a child laboriously pounding out the quarter notes, then an accomplished pianist, then Mozart spiraling off free improvisations on the tune (really!) and again you are listening to music, rather than seeing the page.

There is an essential discontinuity between written music and sounded music. What is accuracy? Accuracy to the page is not music, because the page is a vast oversimplification of the sound. The accuracy must be to the "idea" of the piece, to the "outline" of the song. A reproduction of the page is not listenable music.

The easiest error for a nonmusician to fall into when conversing with a musician is to assume that the symbol equals the object, that a written "A" is an end in itself. The musician constantly seeks the variables, asking: Who? Where? When? How? Why?

If I carry this thought into church, two conclusions are inescapable. The first is that the musicians are obviously the people to ask these questions and to make decisions about musical matters. They do so with respect for their materials and craft, in love for their people and place. The situation in many churches where it is counted democratic to let anyone influence the music program is an absurdity. We don't let the church plumbing or counseling be handled by people with no experience in the field. Why should music be different?

The second conclusion is that the statement "I just want the people to enjoy singing; it doesn't matter how they sound" is meaningless. Music *is* sound, and the better it sounds, the better it is—and the more people will be caught by it.

Singing is the most human, most companionable of the arts. It joins us together in the whole realm of sound, forging a group identity where there were only individuals and making a communicative statement that far transcends what any one of us could do alone. It is a paradigm of union with the creator. It is what the words talk about. We *need* to sing well.

The only way of "mastering" one's material is to abandon the whole conception of mastery and to cooperate with it in love: Whosoever will be a lord of life, let that one be its servant. . . . The business of the creator is not to escape from his material medium or to bully it, but to serve it; but to serve it he must love it.

—Dorothy Sayers

5

A Brief History of Melody

Are you ever curious about a melody's history?

CHURCH MUSICIAN: *Why do I have to know history? Can't I just sing?*

Yes, if you've heard the song well sung. No, if you are a song leader who provides that first hearing for others.

Isn't it enough for me to sing what's on the page?

No, because there are so many values that can't be notated. A song's "style" is an elusive concept. We recognize its presence by being caught in the song. It communicates. And the lack of style communicates negatively, in boredom.

You mean the singer controls whether the music is boring or not?

Almost completely. If the singer knows the song and projects it in love, the listener responds to the love and joins in the song.

How does knowing history help that process?

It provides a context into which to set the melody. If we have heard African or Caribbean or Japanese songs, we bring an ear knowledge to the page. That allows us to re-create those symbols into living sound. The same is true of composers: A Bach phrase sounds different from Mozart or Stravinsky.

Should we always try to sing the song the way it was first sung?

Not necessarily. The process is rather like a game of 20 questions. We ask the tune: Who are you? Where are you from? When and how were you used? What vocal or instrumental music do I know from that time and place which will help me to re-create you?

But then we can change it?

Actually, there's no way we can reproduce it exactly. If we know its style and function, we can make wise choices about how to perform it. We must have respect for the melody as it is before we transform it into another style. It is easy to trivialize a melody by singing it in an unsuitable way; people do it all the time.

Was it always this difficult?

Not at all. In oral cultures, people sang in the style of their own time and place. There was no conflict; everyone knew the prevailing sound. But we live in a shrinking world: Different cultures live side by side. And we are fascinated by history, by the sounds of composers who lived long ago. Mozart's music performed in a dull or inappropriate style simply doesn't satisfy. Any discussion of style has to go far beyond what is written on the page.

And I used to think that there was only one way to perform a piece!

It's almost the opposite. It's truly impossible to perform it the same way twice.

WHAT FOLLOWS is the briefest possible overview of music history, focusing on melody alone. If you think of music as a part of people's everyday lives, you will realize that anything you know about different periods and places will enhance this outline. Music reflects people's lives in the same way that clothes, buildings, tasks, amusements and ways of worship do.

Note: Information on all examples can be found on page 120.

100–1400 Early Period. The priests, the choir and the communicants in the monastery or convent lived the liturgy, accumulating a body of chant that, because the system of notation developed there, became the wellspring of Western music: pure melody.

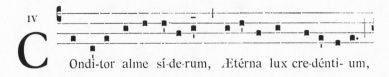

IV

C

Ondi-tor alme sí-de-rum, Ætérna lux cre-dénti- um,

1400–1600 The Reformation. The gift of song was
given to the congregation. The singing of the psalms
and of thousands of "hymns and spiritual songs"
flooded Europe, spurred by the vision of Luther, Calvin
and other skilled musicians and poets. Melodies were
rhythmic, light and quick, in Renaissance style. Voices
and instruments were equal partners, answering each
other with complex interweaving.

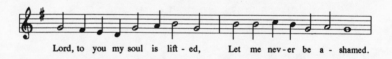

Lord, to you my soul is lift-ed,   Let me nev-er be a-shamed.

At the same time, in the Roman churches, we get
the flowering of the Mass settings from composers like
Palestrina, Victoria and Byrd. The poetry of the Latin
text is united with a music that still speaks to us today
because its function was to foster a transcendence, not
only to accompany specific gestures or texts.

1600–1750 Baroque Period. Johann Sebastian Bach is the towering example here: the composer most universal of all, who took the old hymn tunes (*Choralen,* in German) and set them in the new language of harmony for congregations, organ preludes, cantatas and oratorios, precisely for everyday use in the church. The sound is richer, fuller, but still with the contrapuntal flow of the Renaissance.

1750–1820 Classical Period. Mozart and Haydn provide the standard. Both active in the Roman church, they wrote long and short Masses, expressing the text anew in the balanced and elegant classic style. Orchestras played in the ornate Viennese churches and what the people heard was the same musical language as in symphonies and chamber music. At the same time, in the Protestant churches, Isaac Watts (1674–1748) and Charles Wesley (1707–1788) contributed thousands of strong hymn texts sung to tunes possessing the same grace and clarity. No one could have longed to sing "the good old hymns" then: Congregations must have awaited new songs with the kind of anticipation our society extends to the latest pop ballad.

Je - sus shall reign wher - e'er the___ sun

1820–1900 Romantic Period. The composers were interested in the grand statement, the huge orchestra, the long and complex structure, a rich, emotional, harmonic language free of liturgical or congregational constraints. The sacred music of this period was not written for liturgical use: It is concert music. The church continued to need service music. With great composers otherwise employed, this gap was filled by writers who knew their own traditions but were relatively untrained in the larger craft of poetry or music. They created tunes and texts that are much loved but not of the same quality as the best of previous generations. When there was singing in Catholic parishes, it tended toward imitations of the grand Choral Masses. Yet in some countries of Europe and in some ethnic parishes in the United States, vernacular hymns were popular both at liturgy and in daily life.

Holy, ho - ly, ho - ly Lord God Al - might - y

Outdoor revival songs, like gospel hymns, were easily written and learned, with much repetition and memorable refrains. The "Battle Hymn of the Republic" is an example that everyone knows.

The other strong input into hymnody in the nineteenth century was from folk melodies newly adapted for use as hymns. We keep rediscovering hymns of lasting value from the American frontier.

What won-drous love is this, O my soul, O my soul?

African American spirituals have profoundly influenced the sound of the twentieth century. With their unique blend of African and European idioms, born in suffering but singing of freedom, they provide a new wealth of melody in sacred songs, work songs and love songs.

There___ is a balm in Gil - e - ad To

make the wound - ed whole,___

This trend persists to this day, with our new interest in African, Asian and Latin American hymnody.

Je - su,_____ Je - su,_____ fill

us with your love, show us how to serve

1900–Present. This century, with its multiplicity of styles, has witnessed a simultaneous enthronement and debunking of intellectuality (from dodecacaphony to hard rock), a similar hallowing and rejection of the past (from Telemann to electronic beeps) and a still romantic notion of the separation of art from craft. In the Protestant churches, melody was proclaimed dead; one fashion supplanted another with monotonous regularity (at one moment all the old hymns were thrown out of the church, and at the next, long-forgotten songs were disinterred with full academic honors). Meanwhile, melody continued to live, people continued to sing, and poets and composers were once again "allowed" to write communicative and moving works. Roman Catholics, after Vatican II, entered vigorously into all the peaks and valleys of these times.

Now, in the last decade of the century, there is a heartening increase in the number of composers who don't view religious music as a tiny footnote to music history and who are evolving a language for church music that embraces the congregation as well as the trained artist. And there are congregations who sing lovingly and well. Wherever there is a musically gifted, intuitive, singing organist or choir director, pastor or lay leader, one who loves song and people and is determined to bring them together, it has always happened. And it always will.

When natural music is sharpened and polished by art, then one begins to see with amazement the great and perfect wisdom of

God in this wonderful work of music, where one voice takes a simple part and around it sing three, four or five other voices, leaping, springing round about, marvelously gracing the simple part, like a square dance in heaven with friendly bows, embracings and hearty swinging of the partners. Those who do not find this an inexpressible miracle of the Lord are truly clods and not worthy to be considered human.

—Martin Luther

CHAPTER

6

Studying and
Teaching

The first things are melody, melody, melody.

CHURCH MUSICIAN: *Why do you put so much emphasis here and so little on harmony or accompaniment?*

Because melody has been the neglected portion for some centuries. Harmony took precedence from the Baroque period to the end of the nineteenth century.

But harmony is primarily an adjunct of melody. It doesn't stand well alone.

But hymns sound so bare—so lonely—without the setting.

That's because we don't sing the melody well. Think of those moments when you have heard a great singer without accompaniment: Jessye Norman with a spiritual, or Jean Redpath with a Scottish folk song. What incredible human communication goes on when all the artistry must be confined to a single strand of song.

That takes a wonderful singer.

But we are all designed to sing in that way: Our voices are the primary musical instrument. Our first relationship with a melody should try to answer the question: "How can I sing this song with only my voice (imperfect as it is) and give myself great pleasure?"

Can anybody learn to do that?

Of course, if they learn to listen well enough and to focus their whole being on the song.

But are they really singing for themselves?

That's the first step. Then they should enlarge the focus: "Can I sing so that it gives someone else great pleasure?" A child, perhaps, or a sympathetic friend—I'm not talking about a recital.

But isn't that where this is leading? Isn't that the soloist singing for an audience?

Not in my way of thinking, because the final step for me is to sing in such a way that it encourages others to move beyond listening to responding vocally, joining in. For this, you must become a student of melody, then a performer and then a teacher. And there is no way to disconnect the three roles from one another. They are all one.

A SONG DOES NOT EXIST until it is sung, or re-created, by a human voice. Every incarnation is different and no one sound is the only right one. This is a paradox. A page of music seems to present a finished product, yet it contains no sound. (Hold it up to your ear: Can you hear it?) The song doesn't live until it comes off the page and resumes its natural state as sound. The page can no more substitute for living sound than a recipe can for edible food.

The only sound a song can make is the sound you bring to it this moment. A trained voice will sound different from an untrained, a child's from an adult's, a group's from a soloist's. How you sing the melody becomes the real question.

Articulation is the name for these differences. It has to do with how a note is begun, continued and ended, and its relationship to the notes on either side. Notes can be connected (legato, as in chant) or sharply separated (staccato, as in a xylophone) or anything in between, changing constantly. They can be loud or soft, fierce or gentle, resonant or thin, and a thousand other things. These differences are easily heard but not so easily written on the page.

ONE OF MY FAVORITE definitions of music is: "Music is that which cannot be notated."

As a composer, I believe that all I can notate is five percent of what I hear; the performer must bring the other 95 percent to the page. The performer must be correct to the idea of the song, the pattern of notes and rhythms, phrases and words as they communicate physical, mental, emotional and spiritual qualities in one whole.

But what does music communicate? This is a question that has perplexed philosophers from Plato onward. My answer is "mood"—but this is immediately open to the misconstruction "mood music." The latter seems to me to be something to do something else to, music not meant to be listened to but, almost the opposite, to forget about. Elevator music. Supermarket music. Airport music. Church music. Our society is full of it, and it is doing something deadly to music. We don't listen.

No, my use of "mood" relates to something different, a means of tapping the deep level at which we are all connected. Mood in this sense is the outward part, the audible part, of inward and shared states of being. There is no reason for music unless it communicates, and it should communicate to our minds, hearts and spirits. Sound is one of the most compelling ways to help us drop our defenses, share in our common humanity, rejoice together, mourn together, share each other's quiet and shouting, prayer and praise. Our music schools overemphasize the mental response; our public schools, the visual; our churches, the emotional or mood music side. We rightly crave the whole: to be moved to transcendence, to be united with the song and each other and all God's creation.

IN STUDYING THE SONG, we gradually begin to sense the mood that is being transmitted by that combination of tones, rhythms and text. Often it will run counter to what the words are saying.

Come, O Thou Trav - el - er___ un - known,___ whom still___ I hold,___ but can - not see

If the words and music are transmitting different messages, and we want to sing the song, we must go with the musical message. There is no way that the music can totally submit to the words and still make its point. If we don't like the combination, we shouldn't sing it! We should either read the text or find a new tune that pleases us more.

Come, O Thou Trav-el - er un - known, whom__
still I hold, but can - not __ see

Another hazard is the combination of text and tune that seems to fit the mood and meter but is actually contradictory, demeaning both elements.

How beau - teous were the marks di - vine, that
in thy meek - ness used to shine?

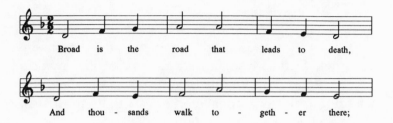

Broad is the road that leads to death,

And thou - sands walk to - geth - er there;

Hymnals are full of such combinations, and becoming sensitive to them is a wonderful way to begin to attune the ear to the subtleties of the text-tune relationship. The contrary, unfortunately, is also true. Singing words and music that do not fit well together dulls that faculty. The sound and the mood *are* connected. It's not that there is just one sound, or one mood, for a song. There are hundreds of possibilities, which change with each singer, each time, each place. The only requirement is that the singer be totally convincing—that he or she has entered the world of the song and is creating it new, here, now.

We must own the song, become the song, to transmit it whole. If I am singing, I must first of all convince myself—that is, be wholly committed to the song, listening with my inner and outer ears to its subtleties, its nonverbal message, its context. My focus, my listening to myself, invites the attention of the listener: "This is important. Listen. Listen to the humor, or the dance, or the longing that is being expressed. Join in. Join in the mood, the sound. Join in the song, as well."

HOW TO SING the melody: That is the first task. The second is to discover to whom I am singing. Who is listening, responding, joining in? Or, to state it the other way: How well do I listen? Can I respond? Can I sing the tune after hearing it once? Can I imitate it exactly? Almost? (It's the only way to prove that I listened.)

Can I make the song my own? Vary it? Answer it? Can I capture those unnotatable elements that are the music? Can I continue the chain and transmit the song to another listener/responder? Can I remember the song? Notating it imprisons it. Can I remove it entirely from the page and restore it to life in this place, immediately, here, now? Can I transmit the affect of the song?

There is a difference between the way I sing a song to myself and to someone else. In the second situation, I adapt my presentation to the listener—a child, a friend, a dinner party, a congregation. It is different each time.

The third task is to sing in a way that invites participation. This is crucial to the song leader; it makes the difference between success or failure. Imagine a superb soloist holding a large audience in rapt attention. Now try to imagine the difference in a leader's attitude that would invite those same listeners to join in. There's no difference in the notes and rhythms, or in the sound and mood—but an enormous change in focus. Rather than singing to the listeners, one is singing with them, submerging one's voice in the sound of the whole, offering the song as a magnet that attracts every ear and voice.

As a leader, I often feel at the beginning as if silence is a chasm between me and the congregation that can only be bridged by song. We are each alone. Can we all be united by the power of the song? As the first, often faint sounds come from my throat, I'm beginning to spin a web connecting me to the group, and my whole effort is to get connecting threads coming back from them. As the song builds, the thread becomes a line, a rope, a cable, a bridge—and finally, there is no division. We are all one in the song.

What then shall I say of the voice of

human beings, to which naught else may be

compared? The heathen philosophers have

striven in vain to explain how the tongue can

express the thoughts of the heart in speech

and song, through laughter and lamentation.

Music is to be praised as second only to

the word of God because by music are all the emotions swayed. Nothing on earth is more mighty to make the sad happy and the happy sad, to hearten the downcast, mellow the overweening, temper the exuberant, or mollify the vengeful. The Holy Spirit itself pays tribute to music when it records that the evil spirit of Saul was exorcised as David played upon his harp.

—Martin Luther

7

A Different
View of the
Hymnal

Do you see any problems with your congregation's hymnal?

CHURCH MUSICIAN: *So many hymns are dated.*

In what way?

All that archaic language, for one thing.

You think it should all be changed?

Well, maybe not the most familiar ones—but so many use old-fashioned theology, terms and images.

"Thee's" and "thy's" are certainly old-fashioned, but so will our wholesale changes appear in a few generations. What we need are new hymns, written in modern American usage, which are sensitive to the issues of inclusive language, contemporary life and theology. The trouble with changing the old ones is the loss of the poetry.

Isn't the theology more important than the poetry?

Oh dear! What an unpoetic time we live in. Theology is expressed in words. Poetry is the art of combining words. In poetry, the sounds, the rhythms, the structure, the images are the work. Good theology does not make a good hymn. A poetic use of words may.

What about the music? All those old tunes . . .

The same kind of thinking is at work. A tune may be "modernized" by changing from the original modal scale to a tonal framework.

Or a changing meter may be compressed into orderly quarter-notes.

And harmonizations keep changing, as successive generations think that new chords, or transposing the hymn up for the last verse, will really transform the tune. It does, in a way: It locks it into a nineteenth-century harmonic framework where chromaticism and modulation are a way of life.

What's wrong with that? I love those rich sounds.

There's nothing wrong with it if it suits the tune. What I object to is making all the tunes sound the same. That is exactly what happens in church after church.

Is historical purity that important?

No. Music is that important, and it's possible. Think how children pick up inflections they hear and how expressive those folksingers are who may not be able to read music.

Are you implying that reading music causes the problem?

It sounds backwards, I know, but unmusical reading makes the tune fit the page. Instead, the page should remind us of wonderfully alive music.

So we should scrap the hymnal and just sing by ear?

The fault is not in the book but in how we use it.

IN THE YEARS I was working as an arranger for the Robert Shaw Chorale, I gained a great respect for melodies that last. It is relatively easy to make a good arrangement of a great tune: Stay out of its way. But many tunes just don't work. Those can be made interesting or unusual or can be covered up with special effects, but these only momentarily disguise the hollowness within.

In the midst of my research for Robert Shaw, I came to look at the hymnal—any hymnal—with entirely new eyes. Here was a collection of tunes that last, a historical anthology of great melodies. Instead of thinking "how harmonically boring" or "how old-fashioned," I tried to put myself in the position of the creator of the hymn. What experience could have led someone to write an ecstatic text like "Holy, holy, holy"? How does it relate to its time and place? The same questions should be asked of the composer of a tune like Duke Street.

Writing either the words or music of a hymn is one of the greatest challenges possible. That tiny form, all self-enclosed: How does one get the words in a natural flow, expressing a cogent idea in language that is rich with the images of scripture, which are really the images of human life? How does one get a tune in which not one note is out of place?

There is also a difference between words and music suitable for communal use and those designed for individuals. The latter may be colloquial; the former must have a breadth of viewpoint, a certain dignity of phrase and basic simplicity of outline. These make it suitable for group utterance.

OUR SOCIETY has not fostered this genre in either poetry or music. We emphasize individuality in every way possible, unwilling to relinquish the slightest iota for the common good. Our use of English in textbooks tends toward a flat, unmusical language. Perhaps to balance this, much daily speech is cliché-ridden, sentimental and ungrammatical. How can meaningful new responses, litanies, psalms or hymns rise out of such language?

Try looking at the three parts of a hymn as if you had written the text, composed the melody and made the setting. Be aware of the implications of each. Do they come from the same place and time, or is there a mixture? Have they already been changed or adapted? Can you find the original? Are there more verses? Were they rearranged in order? Are there different versions of the tune? What is the earliest? Was the setting made by the composer? Has it been adapted?

The small print on the page will give you some of the answers, and the companion volume to the hymnal will give many more. Make your congregation aware of what you have learned. People become fascinated with the history embedded in this familiar book.

The page gives the raw material for performance: the text, the tune and one possible setting. The challenge is the translation into sound of those marks on the page. How do you speak the text meaningfully? Sing the tune so that no one escapes its pull? Perform the setting so that it enhances the melody?

One danger is an excessive literalness: making verses sound the same because they look the same. Subtle variations in dynamics, tempo, mood and articulation cannot be notated—yet they make the song live.

Think for a moment about our use of the organ to introduce and accompany singing in church. It produces sound in a very different way from the voice.

Once the key is depressed, the sound cannot vary unless the registration is changed. In contrast, the human voice is almost unable to sustain a sound without change. The act of forming consonants and vowels, of accenting syllables, of coloring words and arching over phrases is unbelievably complex.

Moreover, I am convinced that voices and instruments sound at different rates of speed. A good tempo for organ is rarely the best one for voices. A slow tempo that allows voices to flower can sound boring on an organ—that's the reason for all the fast notes in keyboard parts. And voices easily can sing faster than many accompanists can manage. Unfortunately, it is possible for an organ or piano to mirror exactly what is on the page, with no style or flow. Most accompanists offer more than that, but too few are possessed of the genius that stimulates singing, gives effective cues to the voices, supports and encourages without overpowering. The effective accompanist must be composer, conductor, arranger, orchestrator and singer all in one.

A HYMNAL SHOULD EMBODY the heritage and beliefs of the community, balancing the best-loved of the past with worthy new additions. In practice, this is an impossible balance. The rate of change in modern society is so swift and people's perceptions of what is "worthy" so varied, that no one hymnal can possibly satisfy. New hymnals are appearing in profusion, each denomination wrestling with the same problems. What to keep in? What to leave out? Which setting? Inclusive language? Representation of different ethnic groups?

My ideal hymnal would consist of time-tested hymns of many styles in as close to their original form as possible. The fruits of research into denominational heritage would be included. Settings would be for four-part voices, rather than two-hand keyboard, to encourage part-singing. Melodies of folk hymns, spirituals and great unison hymns like "Sine Nomine" would be given in tune only, to encourage diversity of improvised settings. Musicians would judge the music; poets would judge the texts; students of song would judge the text/tune relationship. Theologians and special interest groups could suggest and comment but not have the final decision. It could be called The *Musician's Hymnal* or perhaps *The Unhymnal*. It's an impossible dream, but one that would restore honor to the species and art to the user.

In the past several decades, the renewal of the spiritual life of the church has created a pressing need for new hymnody and liturgical music. This has served as a catalyst for a worldwide outburst of creative liturgical and musical activity of a magnitude perhaps unparalleled since the Reformation. [This hymnal] incorporates many of the riches of this contemporary renaissance . . . [and] is a response to the challenge of the church's mission . . . [in] a changed and changing world.

—Preface, The Hymnal 1982

CHAPTER | **8**

The Song Leader

We need a visible, audible human being to lead the assembly in song.

CHURCH MUSICIAN: *But the organ can surely teach the notes better.*

In a way, the organ teaches the wrong thing: an instrumental approach to sound. It doesn't really model a vocal sound: phrase, line, text.

And you think this articulation is taught by one person singing to and with a group?

It's the only way. It can only be taught by ear. Paradoxically, it is easier to teach an unfamiliar song. People will echo back what they have just heard rather than what they remember or what they see on the page.

And this kind of singing will increase participation?

Certainly. The more music we make, the more it exerts its own magnetic spell, drawing others into it.

Even those that say they can't sing?

Even some of those. There is an immediate reward that is hard to describe to people who haven't experienced it. But let's keep our goals clear. The point is to encourage everyone to join in singing well, because it forges us into one worshiping body in a way that nothing else can do.

THINK OF THE SONG LEADER, the cantor, in light of this description by Rabbi Abraham Joshua Heschel:

The right Hebrew word for cantor is *ba'al tefillah*, master of prayer. The mission of a cantor is to lead in prayer. He does not stand before the Ark as an artist in isolation, trying to demonstrate his skill or to display vocal feats. He stands before the Ark not as an individual but with a congregation. He must identify himself with the congregation. His task is to represent as well as to inspire a community. Within the synagogue music is not an end in itself but a means of religious experience. Its function is to help us to live through a moment of confrontation with the presence of God: to expose ourselves to him in praise, in self-scrutiny and in hope.

The rabbi is teacher; the cantor, master of prayer. That definition, and its extension in the quote above, show clearly the cantor's role. Most of our Christian churches have had someone like this cantor: a Vorsänger, a Praecentor, a song leader at one time or another in their history. We find this from ancient Roman practice to the itinerant revival team on the American frontier—preacher and song leader, riding through the wilderness together.

In essence, a cantor provides a visible/audible model for the assembly. The visual element is of great importance. Light travels swiftly; sound, slowly. A person sitting in the farthest corner of a large church can see the cantor raise an arm at the same microsecond as those in the front row. Hearing a cue from the organ is different. It takes time for the organ pipe to "speak," for that sound to roll through the space—and no singer is going to enter before hearing a sounded cue, making another tiny delay. By the time that farthest voice is sounding, the organ is often on the next note. Acoustical drag is almost unavoidable without a visible leader, although gifted conductor/organists can help people sing together.

Think also of our earliest teaching models for music, before we ever get to school or have a piano lesson. A loved face is inextricably bound up with the song in memory, as it should be. Song comes from human beings to human beings, and the best teaching comes from someone who loves to sing, who loves the song and the assembly and can bring them together.

IN THE PRESENT DAY, Roman Catholic cantors are resuming this function. Since the benefits are so immediate, it seems that all our denominations should have some person, by whatever name, whose function is to lead the group in song. If they do nothing more than stand, facing the people, singing with heart and voice, face and body, they are giving a visual image of how each individual should participate.

The addition of a gracious gesture to include all the congregation, or to give a gentle cutoff, helps the music. Other gestures should be unobtrusively welcoming, helping each individual to focus on the song. The cantor should have a true voice but not necessarily a trained one—the aim is to get people to join in, and too "professional" a voice may accomplish just the opposite. Most of all, through face and body language, cantors must show contact with and sympathy for each individual in the group.

I have heard the objection to cantorial gesture that it distracts the worshiper. The question here is one of priorities: Do we want good singing? Somehow it must be taught, led, encouraged. If the song is well chosen and well sung, it will add immeasurably to the liturgy.

THE ORIGINAL FUNCTION of the Vorsänger or Praecentor—the "Before-Singer"—was
to teach the song in the absence of both accompaniment and hymnal. This leader would sing one line
with the congregation repeating, then the next, and so
on to the end. Carried through several verses, this can
become tedious, but for one verse it is the most efficient way I know to teach a new hymn. One voice is
providing the model for each individual listening,
teaching the whole (pitch, rhythm, text, mood,
dynamics, affect) without extraneous material (harmony or accompaniment) to confuse the listener.

Playing the hymn on the organ or having the choir
sing it through does not accomplish the same thing.
A group of voices doesn't provide the model for one
voice. The cantor alone can best work in phrases.
A phrase is "a memorable unit"—anything longer is
too much to remember. And no instrument can cope
with words—a prime responsibility of the model.
Accompaniment does not help the congregation sing
better. Sometimes it gives them a convenient excuse:
The music will continue whether we sing or not.

We need to train people in this expanded role of song leader. For too long we have relied on the organ, the choir and the hymnal to "make it easy" for the group to sing. In the absence of a singing tradition, that simply doesn't work. This teaching needs to be done at every opportunity: in Sunday school, at social gatherings, at open sings, at choir rehearsals, at home, before the service, after the service and during the service. Do we want good singing? I don't know any better way to get it.

Who, in your church, would be the best song leader? It might be the music director, or the minister, or a teacher of young people, or a member of the assembly. This person must love to sing and to teach and to learn, continually trying different ways to involve everyone in this spiritual discipline. There are wonderful "Directions for Singing" by John Wesley (found in *The Methodist Hymnal*), which address in plain English the responsibilities of the singer.

> Learn these tunes.
> Sing all. . . . If it is a cross to you, take it up,
>   and you will find it a blessing.
> Sing lustily and with a good courage.

Sing modestly.
Sing in time.
Above all sing spiritually.

HERE ARE SOME SUGGESTIONS for song leaders. Know yourself. Know what tunes you really respond to, and why. Keep enlarging your own repertory. Collect hymnals, tune books, service music, great choral music, all kinds of music. Be a student of melody and learn from the tunes. Find which ones work in group settings and how to present them. What is the music saying, without any words?

Know your hymnal. Know all of it. Read all the verses of all the hymns, and all the versions of the service music. Sing all the tunes without accompaniment. Can you hold your own attention? Someone else's? A child's? Know other versions of the songs in your hymnal and where to look up their earliest forms. Be aware how different a tune can sound with a new text, and vice versa. Most of all, be aware of the mood that is set by this particular tune and text. Make new indexes of the music in your hymnal: historical, mood, function (march, lullaby, square dance), manner of peformance (rounds, guitar songs, improvisatory).

Know your congregation. Keep a list of which songs they sing each week, noting their collective and individual likes and dislikes. Learn ways to introduce new tunes that predispose people to want to sing them. Constantly increase the variety of tunes that your congregation knows, maintaining a balance of different styles. Learn how to choose the music for a service. It may be of one period or of many, but it needs to interrelate with itself and with the service as a whole. Choosing by text is not enough. The tunes need to add their own voices.

Know how to teach a song. How do you choose a pitch, a tempo, a mood? What do you teach first? If you start with bare notes and rhythms, you will surely lose the group's attention before you get to "expression." Pitch it high enough so that good voices are comfortable and so that lower parts will be sung. Teach it at the right tempo, not slower or faster. Set your mood and hold to it. Your main concern is to make the song live, not to make it correct.

Use your own most natural, expressive voice.
Sing lightly, so you can reflect the most subtle curves
of text, pitch and rhythm. Vary the tone for different
tunes: "endless, subtle variation" is nature's law.
Require the group to sing lightly. I call this "listening-
singing" and it's the opposite of the football cheer.
Loudness is not an end in itself. I spend much time
quieting people down so that they hear themselves and
each other.

If you teach one verse carefully—to establish
just the right tempo and tone, mood and function—
you have set up a kind of momentum that should carry
through the song. Sing the rest of the verses without
lining-out, but maintain sensitivity to tone and text.
By your attitude, keep inviting everyone in the room to
participate, from young to old, from accomplished
musicians to beginners.

Above all, teach the whole. Demonstrate what you
want to hear, in listening, focus, sound, appreciation
of text. Go for the "sound in the room," the sound
being made right now, here, that would be different if
one person left or another entered. Listen so intently
that you make everyone hear better. Respond so

openly to the suggestions of text and tune that you increase everyone's awareness. Set the mood and keep it. Find the sound, and don't let it go. This is what unites the people in true singing worship.

There are hardly proofs for the existence of God, but there are witnesses. Foremost among them are the Bible and music. Our liturgy is a moment in which these two witnesses come to expression. "On the evidence of two witnesses a claim is sustained." Our liturgy consists of the testimony of both music and the word. Perhaps this is the way to define a ba'al tefillah. He is a person in whom the two witnesses meet. He is a person in whom a spiritual equation takes place—the equation of song and soul, or word and mind. The self and prayer are one.

—Abraham Joshua Heschel

CHAPTER | **9**

Collaboration
in the
Community

Who chooses the music for your service?

CHURCH MUSICIAN: *Everybody seems to be an expert at that.*

And they don't hesitate to tell you.

Exactly! Music seems to be an area where everyone not only knows a style but is sure that that's the only path for the whole program to take.

And your professional competence doesn't seem to count for much.

No, I seem to be one voice among equals—and an outnumbered one at that.

It's a real concern. Professional integrity in the arts often seems not to count in our churches. Some musicians are fortunate enough to be in communities that share their values, but others are hounded almost beyond belief by people who should know better.

I LEARNED ABOUT the value of collaboration during my 20 years of work with Robert Shaw on the arrangements that bear both our names. In every case, the result of our working together was more imaginative, tightly constructed and communicative than either of us could have produced alone. Since then I have discovered the joys of planning a service with a preacher who is as eager as I to join words and music in meaningful worship. We each respect the other's expertise, trading suggestions, bartering, compromising, until we come up with a plan that suits the occasion and the people, one much better than either of us could have achieved alone.

In our churches, ordained ministers and nonordained leaders, choir members, religious education teachers and members of the community should be engaged in a continuing, creative dialogue with the music staff. We musicians cannot work in isolation. Indeed, the very communal nature of music places a particular responsibility on us to be responsive to the people around us. Too often, misconceptions about music's role in the church make life uncomfortable, if not unbearable, for the true musician. I had one friend who left a position in church music, saying: "Never was I challenged to do my best. I love my church, and I love music, but I just couldn't work there."

We need to be better teachers, communicators and evangelists for our beliefs. We need to be both diplomatic and strong in standing up against elements that trivialize music. We are the ones who must stand up for ear values, for music's right to sound, for non-rational and nonvisual elements in worship. Above all, we need mutual respect with our co-workers in both art and craft.

Pastors are the heads of individual parishes. Their attitudes toward music will set the tone for the whole body: If they love to sing, so will the congregation. If they regard music as an "aid to worship," something to fill the spaces between the words, then the congregation gets an inescapable signal that music is not important, and even the best musicians become discouraged.

We get a similar scenario from strong-minded parishioners who know what kind of music is best for the congregation. They believe that if we just sang

1. all the "good-old hymns"
2. only new and upbeat
3. loud and fast
4. slowly and reverently

or some such directive for our repertory, then all our problems would be solved.

From the other side, we can list the beliefs of the professionally trained musician who is determined to "raise the level" of music in the parish, and who demands

1. only Bach Chorales
2. only music before 1800

3. only music before 1600
4. only music by post-1960s composers

The main thing that is troubling about these scenarios is their limited vision. They cut off the wonderful variety of sound that is our heritage. In such situations, musicians in the church may feel bereft. Who is standing up for music: for pitch and rhythm, for phrase and articulation, for text-tune relationships, for choral tone, and for the community that is established in their presence?

There can be rivalry between the organist and the choir director, schism within the field. Historically, voices came first, but when instruments came into church, they did tend to take over. Our wholesale endorsement of the organ as the instrument of sacred music is a curious one, given its expense, its problems of placement, balance and repair, and the great skill that is needed to play it musically. There needs to be respect on both sides of this equation, and preferably similar taste and goals, for it to work well. For good congregational singing, the voice must come first, and the organist must learn to play in a way that encourages singing.

ONE SIDE OF the choir's function shows a loyal giving of time and talent to the church. The other side can be too involved with performance and with separation from the assembly. The Puritans forbade choirs. They do remove the best voices from the congregation, and there are choir members all over the country who have never been next to their families during the liturgy. Maybe some rethinking is in order.

As for the children and their religious education programs, for far too long there has been a chasm between what the adults sing and what the children are taught. A plethora of "hymnals for children" have appeared with original ditties or watered-down versions of hymns. I remember one version of "All creatures of our God and king" with the phrase "Thou burning sun" changed to "Thou shining sun" because "burning" might disturb the children. What are we doing? These are the adults of 20 years hence. Will they know the heritage, sing the great hymns as they should be sung, join in the liturgy with heart and voice and mind?

The choir director of the adults should supervise the children's musical activities, and the children should be prepared each week to sing hymns with the adults in the coming Sunday's liturgy. I'm sure that I learned to read by following my mother's finger as it moved along the lines of the hymnal. We should see this active teaching taking place everywhere small children are present—rather than isolating them by age or ignoring their presence.

THE BENEFITS of these kinds of collaboration should be evident. It takes time to develop this and all need to approach their work with the spirit of conciliation and compromise. It's much easier and far more efficient to have one person dictate and the others carry out orders. But think of the learning potential of the people who have a stake in the results, who become ardent participants in the music program because they have been asked, and have given of themselves, have contributed to the life of the assembly and its liturgy.

Collaboration with respect. The musician's task is to stand up for music's right to communicate on its own terms, not just as a background to words or actions. A congregation's ability to sing well their responses, acclamations and hymns is the first step toward their becoming adept in the spiritual disciplines of music.

You must know that the Holy Spirit, in order

to cause a soul to advance in spirituality . . .

educates the hearing before coming to the

vision. Listen, my child, he says, and see . . .

Only the hearing attains to truth because it

perceives the Verb. And thus one must awaken

the hearing and train it to receive the truth.

—St. Bernard

CHAPTER | **10**

Sounding

Space

What are some of the things that you have no control over and that limit your work?

CHURCH MUSICIAN: *Our building, for one. The design, the immovable furniture, placement of the organ and choir loft, the acoustics.*

Almost everyone shares these problems. There's really no such

thing as an ideal space, and musicians' thoughts are apt
to be very different from other key people.

*What can I do about the bad sight lines and acoustics
in my situation? The organist has to use a mirror
to see the choir, and neither one can really hear the
other.*

I'd suggest that you draw a diagram that illustrates the
difficulty. No one else will think of it from your point
of view, so you have to make it clear.

Then what?

Try enlisting others to help you think through what
might be changed.

But we can't relocate the organ!

Perhaps the choir doesn't have to be in the choir loft.
Could that space be used for seating latecomers?
(I'm only half joking!) Couldn't the choir members sit
with their families and come together for the few
"choir only" pieces?

That sounds much too informal.

And do you need to use the organ all the time? We
are apt to think of the loss of the instrument through

repair or replacement as a catastrophe. In some places this "catastrophe" has been a wonderful opportunity to get people to sing.

My congregation thinks the organ is essential. I tried leaving it out for one verse; people rushed up afterwards to find out what was the matter.

You need to let them know ahead of time what you are planning to do.

How about the acoustics? There's no "bloom" to the sound coming from the congregation.

Are there carpets? Seat cushions? Curtains? Acoustical tiles? The basic problem for musicians is the lack of faith in, or knowledge of, sound by the architects and decorators and redecorators of our churches. They put their faith in technology, thinking they can fix things with electronics. But it can't be done.

Nor can I do a festival service if the choir is in the balcony at one end of the church and the only place for the instruments is at the other end. How I wish we could have adaptable spaces!

WHAT WE ARE TALKING about here is part of a larger problem. We need to think of the liturgy as a whole, involving all of our senses, bodies, minds and hearts.

When we read a play, we are holding in our hands the material written by the playwright on which the production will be founded. But the page isn't the play until it has been brought to life by human beings. Story, characterization, language, staging are indicated in the text, but they have to be reinterpreted for each new production. It is possible to be very faithful to the page, or wildly imaginative, but there is no way to do it without making hundreds of decisions that either add up to a communicative performance or a dull one.

For instance, one of the glories of drama is that it can make us totally forget where we are sitting. Often the most imaginative productions are in the least well-equipped situations, and the most moving drama in bare surroundings.

So it is with our churches. We tend to get used to the way they look and sound. If we think through our worship experience from the point of view of someone participating for the first time, perhaps we can get resensitized to possibilities that are dormant.

What kind of building are you in? How does it "sound"? How does the organ sound from different locations? How are sight lines? Lighting? (Enough to read the small print in the hymnal?) What gestures and motions are used? Do they change from time to time? Are people prepared for their participation? What do they wear? How do they stand, sit, move, speak, sing? How about children? What hymnal and/or worship aids are used? What impression does your bulletin give to a visitor? What visual and audial impression does the processional really make? (Make a videotape and find out.) Would you look and listen with delight if you didn't know the participants? Why should it seem more "true" if it looks and sounds unrehearsed?

Is it obvious that liturgy is something people sing? Are responses and acclamations a recognizable part of the whole? Does everyone participate? Is there enough singing at one time to get voices warmed up and ears listening? What is the mood at the beginning? The end? Is there a reasonable balance of sound and silence, motion and stillness, emotion and thought?

One of the great dramatic values is silence. In our radio/TV age we've almost forgotten this. How awake are our eyes and ears when our minds are not being told what to see or listen for? How often do we tell in the bulletin, on the wall, and by announcement what the next hymn is, when any one way would suffice? How often do we announce "Please rise" when a gesture would be more gracious?

IN OUR MUSIC, it's not so much the "art" as the "craft"—the attention to each detail, the wish to get it just right, to make it a unified whole, matching intention with doing. In liturgical services there are wonderful patterns, tested over centuries. The congregation has an important part to play. If it doesn't know its lines, if it is insecure or inaccurate in performance, there is no chance for the right meaning to be present. Why are we so afraid of rehearsal? Repeating a brief response several times until it is "set" will ensure good performance thereafter. There is a memory to return to. If the ideal never has been clearly achieved, the same muddiness will persist, week after week, and become harder and harder to change.

There's no way to make music without performing, playing, practicing. In the best musical sense, excellent performance is finely tuned, buoyantly rhythmic, intensely communicative, stylistically sensitive, wholly focused, so that the listener is drawn into the sound. It's not enough for an assembly to sing the responses: We need to do them well.

But worship is what we're *doing*, not talking about or thinking about. If we are clear that our music is a gift of God, and we are returning this gift, we have no trouble setting our sights high, raising our expectations and daring to improve as we worship.

The concept of a room alive with sound

was basically related to a religious outlook.

Music was not simply a performance to

which one listened, but rather a manifestation

in sound of the sacred place. The church itself was an architectural hymn of praise to the deity. Believers entered this domain — and when it began to resonate with sound, the sound came not from any specific source, but rather from everywhere, coalesced with the architecture. The awareness of such a sacred space could have an overwhelmingly powerful effect.

—Nikolaus Harnoncourt

C H A P T E R **II**

Sacred Song

There is, of course, no such thing as sacred music.

CHURCH MUSICIAN: *Then what have we been talking about?*

Words can be about sacred or secular matters, but the sound waves themselves can't distinguish between the two. We find wonderful music in all periods that has migrated into the church from secular sources.

But surely there is such a thing as sacred song?

Indeed there is, in intent and in function. It serves our deepest human needs. The point I want to make is that in order to do so, it cannot be less than music. It must partake of the same substance as any great music in order to move us. Whether or not it has sacred words is beside the point.

Are you implying that there is no difference between an art song and a hymn?

As far as the words are concerned, there is. But the music in both is dealing with pitches and rhythms and form and energy. A pious hope is not enough to make the song good music.

But surely music that has been inspired by great religious words is different from dance music!

Song is song. It either works musically or it doesn't. If you say that the church musician doesn't need as much craft as a secular counterpart, we are separating church music from other music and making it less demanding as an art. This is a discussion that has been going on in Western cultures for many centuries. Somehow it doesn't seem to arise in Asian and African societies where the gulf between art and function doesn't exist. Are religion and the arts really opposed? Do they really threaten one another?

Shouldn't we be thinking about God and Christ and salvation as we worship? What are all the words for?

The mystics and the Eastern religions would answer that the words are to help us find the path, the end of which is wordless prayer.

So music equals prayer?

Not all music, and not all prayer. This dichotomy is a product of the modern mind which focuses on divisions rather than unities, on rationalities (words) rather than those uncomfortable concepts like faith, art and spirituality which defy verbal limitations.

Surely "spirituality" means things of the spirit?

Our mistake is to separate body, mind, spirit. We are intended to be whole, holy. The mind can only process materials that have come to it initially through the senses. Then it can collect, remember, categorize and begin to draw connections. The arts are the exaltation of the senses that the Creator gave us. The arts are, for me, the road to God, to "that which *is*." At their best, they provide immediate experiences of light, color, sound, smell, taste and touch: direct gifts of God. It is the questioning, defining, abstracting mind that separates us from primary experience.

Primary?

The ability to let go of the ego, the rationality, and become so open that we truly see, hear, smell, taste, touch—and are touched.

So all the arts are the essence of religion?

They are gifts for us to use. Our society tends to view them as entertainment. Most of the world's cultures refuse to separate them either from daily life or from religion.

And music has a special role?

Music, especially song, is the most human of the arts. It needs no materials or tools other than the ear and throat—along with mind and heart. When we sing alone, we are led out of ourselves into the world of the song. When we sing together, we create a community, a communion in sound. The group becomes more than the sum of its parts: It is creating beauty.

And the better the performance, the greater the communion.

Precisely.

WHAT HAPPENS WHEN this works right is mystical. Writing in *Parabola* magazine about the twelfth-century Cistercian abbey near Le Thoronet in France, Robert Lawlor notes:

> The nave is so sound-sensitive that one becomes aware that every body movement creates an impact on the volume of air in the chamber. Movement can thus be considered to be an inaudible tone; the body, seemingly guided by the reverberation of its own silent sound returned to it from the stone vault, is gradually impelled to move in a quiet, harmonious way. . . .
>
> It is evident that St. Bernard was an inheritor of a very ancient spiritual doctrine, a doctrine that understood that our two chief senses, sight and hearing, affect us in two completely different ways. In a general way, through vision we take in images coming from the apparently external world. The mind reacts through

instinct, habit, memory, association, calculation or reason. But with hearing, sound creates an instantaneous (and mathematically precise) recognition of a tone, without the intervention of mind. At the same time this sound may touch and connect regions of high emotion and mindless knowing.

Imagine your church members filling their space at the beginning of the liturgy. Imagine that all the space in the room is full of the possibility of song. It awaits the first vibration to set it in motion. Until then, the song exists only as a ghostly sphere. Tone sets it moving, expanding, growing, flowering, changing, subsiding, ceasing. The first sound must be exactly right and each succeeding sound must grow inevitably from that beginning.

The singers give up ego, selfhood and control to enter that world of vibration, and by this example and the magnetic quality of pure sound, they induce everyone to join the mystical journey.

The amazing thing is that this can happen every time we sing. All that we have to do is ask for it. It never comes unbidden, but it is always there when we seek it. We are literally "one body" when we sing together in this way. One with each other, one with the physical universe, and one with the Creator who gave us the Song.

And it came to pass, when the priests were come out of the holy place: (for all the priests that were present were sanctified, and did not then wait by course: Also the Levites which were the singers, all of them of Asaph, of Heman, of Jeduthun, with their sons and their brethren, being arrayed in white linen, having cymbals and psalteries and harps, stood at the east end of the altar, and with them an hundred and twenty priests sounding with trumpets:)

It came even to pass, as the trumpeters and
singers were as one, to make one sound to
be heard in praising and thanking the Lord;
and when they lifted up their voice with
the trumpets and cymbals and instruments of
musick, and praised the Lord, saying,

For he is good;
for his mercy endureth for ever:
that then the house was filled with a cloud,
even the house of the Lord; So that the priests
could not stand to minister by reason of the
cloud: for the glory of the Lord had filled the
house of God.

—2 Chronicles 5:11—14

119

Melodious
Accord

MUSIC SOURCES

Folk Hymns of America (Annabel Morris Buchanan). New York: J. Fischer, 1938.

The Hymnal 1982. New York: The Church Hymnal Corporation, 1985.

The Mennonite Hymnal. Newton KS: Faith and Life Press, 1969.

The Methodist Hymnal. Nashville: The Methodist Publishing House, 1964.

The Presbyterian Hymnal. Louisville: Westminster/John Knox Press, 1990.

Worship: A Hymnal and Service Book for Roman Catholics. Chicago: GIA Publications, Inc., 1986.

PAGE 41 · Chant notation for the beginning of the hymn at vespers during Advent.

PAGE 42 · **The Presbyterian Hymnal, #178.** Text: Stanley Wiersma, 1980 (Psalm 25). Tune: Genevan 25, Louis Bourgeois, 1551.
Sung with a quick, even pulse, stressing only accented syllables, which yields a delightfully varied meter:
    (5/8) Lord, to you my (7/8) soul is lifted
    (6/8) Let me never (8/8) be ashamed

PAGE 43 · **Worship, #434.** Text: *Salve caput cruentatum*, Bernard of Clairvaux, tr. Henry Baker. Tune: Passion Chorale, Hans Leo Hassler, 1564–1612; setting: J. S. Bach, 1685–1750.
Hassler's version of the melody was rhythmically varied, as in the previous example (it also had a secular text). Here the melody has been simplified and is sung more slowly to allow the chords to sound.

PAGE 44 · **Worship, #492.** Text: Isaac Watts, 1674–1748, alt. Tune: Duke Street, John Hatton, d. 1793.
This should sound like an elegant, light march: a Mozart string quartet movement.

PAGE 45 · Worship, #485. Text: Reginald Heber, 1783–1826, alt. Tune: Nicea, J. B. Dykes, 1823–1876.

PAGE 46 (top) · Worship, #600. Text: Alexander Means, 1801–1853. Tune: Wondrous Love, *Southern Harmony*, 1835.
This should be slow, with a steady beat and accent: It's a "lonesome tune."

PAGE 46 (bottom) · Worship, #608. Text: African American Spiritual, based on Jeremiah 8:22. Tune: Balm in Gilead, African American Spiritual.
This should be slow, and almost as free in rhythm as the chant in the first example. *Any* harmony that people improvise will sound better than any written-out four-part harmonization.

PAGE 47 · Worship, #431. Text: Ghana Folk Song, based on John 13:3–5; tr. Tom Colvin. Tune: Chereponi, Ghana Folk Song.
The traditional music of Ghana exerted a strong influence on Caribbean songs. Think of this as having a light percussion accompaniment, and the kind of melodious accent that comes from the French islands.

PAGE 57 · The Methodist Hymnal, #529. Text: Charles Wesley, 1742. Tune: Candler.
The Scottish folk song melody has a light, wistful, remembering quality to it: "Thou mindst me of departed joys." Hardly the right companion for Wesley's text.

PAGE 58 (top) · The Mennonite Hymnal, #322. Text: Charles Wesley, 1742. Tune: Vernon, *Christian Harmony*, 1805.
This slow, modal melody can take all the weight of the text.

PAGE 58 (bottom) · The Methodist Hymnal, #80. Text: A. Cleveland Coxe, 1818–1896. Tune: Windham, Daniel Read, 1757–1836.
Note the sentimental text and the tripping triple meter that make the tune seem lightweight.

PAGE 59 · Folk Hymns of America, #10. Text: Isaac Watts, 1674–1748. Tune: Windham, Daniel Read, 1757–1836.
This is the combination of text and tune found in many early American hymnals. The solemn text with its slower tempo and duple meter reveal an inherent nobility in the tune.

PAGE 68 (top) · Folk Hymns of America, #18; The Methodist Hymnal, #129. Tune: Davis (in *The Methodist Hymnal*).
This change happened to many melodies in nineteenth-century America, as the influence of the gospel hymns with their sturdy, major chords pushed out older modal versions.

PAGE 68 (bottom) · The Hymnal 1982, #3 and #310. Tune: *Herr Jesu Christ, Cantional Germanicum*, 1629; setting: J. S. Bach, 1685–1750.
This happened in eighteenth-century Europe, as tonality and the language of harmony supplanted the dance-like rhythms and modes of the Renaissance.